W9-AMU-581

Hockey In Canada

Ottawa Senators

Written by
Don Cruickshank

Published by Weigl Educational Publishers Limited
6325 – 10 Street SE
Calgary, Alberta, Canada
T2H 2Z9

Web site: www.weigl.com

Library and Archives Canada Cataloguing in Publication

Cruickshank, Don
      Ottawa Senators / Don Cruickshank.

(Hockey in Canada)
Includes index.
ISBN 1-55388-262-8 (bound)
ISBN 1-55388-263-6 (pbk.)

     1. Ottawa Senators (Hockey team)--Juvenile literature.
I. Title. II. Series.

GV848.O89C78 2006   j796.962'64097138   C2006-902127-9

Printed in the United States of America
1 2 3 4 5 6 7 8 9 0 10 09 08 07 06

All of the Internet URLs given in the book were valid at the time of publication. However, due to the dynamic nature of the Internet, some addresses may have changed, or sites may have ceased to exist since publication. While the author and publisher regret any inconvenience this may cause readers, no responsibility for any such changes can be accepted by either the author or the publisher.

Every reasonable effort has been made to trace ownership and to obtain permission to reprint copyright material. The publishers would be pleased to have any errors or omissions brought to their attention so that they may be corrected in subsequent printings.

We gratefully acknowledge the financial support of the Government of Canada through the Book Publishing Industry Development Program (BPIDP) for our publishing activities.

Editor
Frances Purslow

Design and Layout
Terry Paulhus

Contents

PAGE 9

PAGE 18

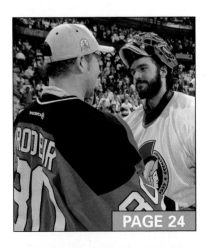

PAGE 24

The History of the NHL

Hockey has been around for many years. Most historians credit James Creighton, a Canadian, with writing the first set of rules for hockey. These rules, called the Halifax Rules, are in the **Hockey Hall of Fame** in Toronto. In 1875, Creighton organized and played in the first official game of ice hockey using these rules. It was played at the Victoria Skating Rink in Montreal. About 18 years later, teams from the **Amateur** Hockey Association of Canada began competing for the **Stanley Cup**, called the Dominion Hockey Challenge Cup at the time. In 1914, the Stanley Cup became the exclusive trophy of two **professional** leagues. These leagues were the National Hockey Association (NHA) and the Pacific Coast Hockey Association (PCHA).

Three years later, the National Hockey League (NHL) was formed out of the NHA. The teams playing in the league at that time were the Montreal Canadiens, the Montreal Wanderers, the Toronto Arenas, and the Ottawa Senators.

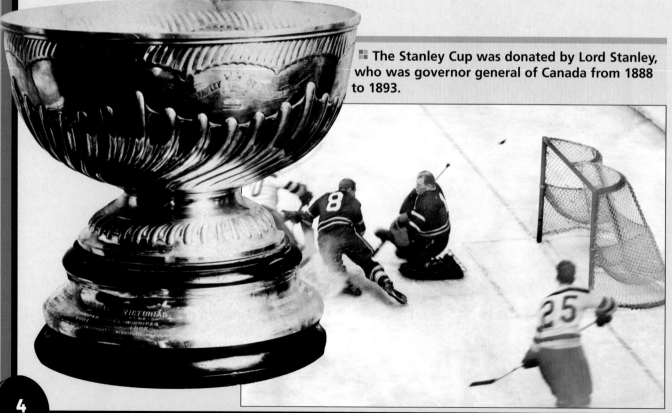

■ The Stanley Cup was donated by Lord Stanley, who was governor general of Canada from 1888 to 1893.

4

Over the next 25 years, several other teams joined and left the NHL. When the **Great Depression** occurred in the 1930s, the Montreal Maroons, the New York Americans, and the original Ottawa Senators withdrew from the league due to a lack of funds. The remaining six teams in the league at the start of the 1942–43 season became known as the Original Six. For the next 25 years, no new teams were allowed into the league, and none of the six teams changed locations. In 1967, the NHL expanded by adding six new **franchises**. Since that time, the league has expanded many times.

Today, there are 30 teams in the NHL. Six are based in Canadian cities, and the other 24 are in the United States. The Canadian NHL teams are the Vancouver Canucks, the Edmonton Oilers, the Calgary Flames, the Toronto Maple Leafs, the Montreal Canadiens, and the Ottawa

THE ORIGINAL SIX

Between the 1942–43 season and the league's expansion in 1967, there were only six teams in the NHL. They were the Montreal Canadiens, the Toronto Maple Leafs, the Detroit Red Wings, the Chicago Blackhawks, the New York Rangers, and the Boston Bruins. They are known as the Original Six.

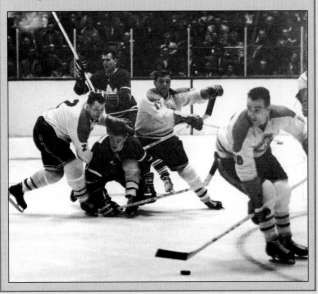

CHANGES THROUGHOUT THE YEARS

PAST	The puck was wooden.	There were seven players per team on the ice.	Forward passes were against the rules.	There were goal posts, but no nets. Goals were scored from either side of the goal line.
PRESENT	The puck is rubber.	There are six players per team on the ice.	Forward passes are allowed.	Nets are used.

5

The Rise of the Ottawa Senators

1917

The NHL is formed. The Ottawa Senators are one of four teams in the NHL. Their jerseys are red, black, and white. Their logo is a black O with red and white trim. The O stands for Ottawa. Their first home arena is the Dey's Arena. It holds 7,000 people. They finish third out of four teams in their first NHL season. They miss the **playoffs**.

1920

The Ottawa Senators move to the Ottawa Arena, also called the Auditorium. They win their first Stanley Cup as an NHL team in their new home arena.

1923

The Ottawa Senators win their sixth Stanley Cup. They defeat the Vancouver Maroons in four games of a best-of-five series, and the Edmonton Eskimos in two games of a best-of-three series. The first NHL hockey broadcasts air on the radio. The play-by-play announcer telephones the radio station, which airs the game from the telephone to the audience.

1927

A new NHL rule allows forward passes. The Senators defeat the Boston Bruins to win the Stanley Cup. This is the first year that only NHL teams are allowed to compete for the Stanley Cup.

1934

The Ottawa Senators are sold to St. Louis. This is because The City of Ottawa can no longer afford to support an NHL franchise. After one season, they fold.

1992

The Ottawa Senators rejoin the NHL in the 1992–93 season. They keep the same name and their red, black, and white team colours. They change their logo to that of a Roman soldier. Their home arena is the Ottawa Civic Centre. They finish last in the league and miss the playoffs.

1993

The Ottawa Senators draft Alexander Daigle first overall in the NHL **Entry Draft**. Daigle is considered to be the next Wayne Gretzky. The Senators again finish last in the league standings and miss the playoffs.

1996

In January, the Ottawa Senators move from the Ottawa Civic Centre to the Corel Centre.

1996–97

The Ottawa Senators qualify for the playoffs for the first time since rejoining the league. They are defeated by the Buffalo Sabres in the first round.

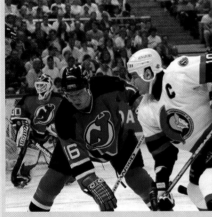

1997–98

The Ottawa Senators win their first playoff series. They defeat the New Jersey Devils in six games. They advance to the second round but lose to the Washington Capitals in five games.

2002–03

The Ottawa Senators finish as the league's best team in the regular season. They win the President's Trophy.

Quick Facts

- Ottawa is the capital of Canada. It is located in the province of Ontario.
- The prime minister's residence is in Ottawa. The address is 24 Sussex Drive.
- Ottawa's population is about 1 million.
- Ottawa is home to the National Gallery of Canada. This gallery features the world's largest collection of Canadian art.

Home of the Senators

The first home arena for the Ottawa Senators was Dey's Arena. It was one of three arenas built by brothers Edwin and William Dey. Edwin was part owner of the Senators and team president from 1918 until 1923. The arena was built in 1907 and was used by the Ottawa Senators until they moved to the Ottawa Arena in 1920.

The Ottawa Senators won the Stanley Cup in the Ottawa Arena in 1927. They continued to play in this arena until 1934, when the team folded. In 1965, the Ottawa Arena was torn down and replaced by the Ottawa Civic Centre.

The Civic Centre was the Ottawa Senators' home arena from 1992 to 1995. The building was built in 1968. It can seat more than 9,800 fans. Over the years, the building has hosted many political events, concerts, and other sporting events. In summer, a zoo and various stores are located there.

The Centre is home to the Ottawa 67's of the Ontario Hockey League (OHL). The OHL features some of the best players in Ontario that are between the ages of 16 and 20. The Civic Centre is located on Bank Street.

> The seat located farthest from the ice surface in Scotiabank Place is only 42 metres away, less than one rink length.

In 1996, the Ottawa Senators moved from the Civic Centre to the Corel Centre. The Ottawa Senators played their first game there on January 17, 1996, against the Montreal Canadiens. Today, the Corel Centre is called Scotiabank Place.

Scotiabank Place has a seating capacity of 18,500. It is located in Kanata, a small city east of Ottawa. The facility cost $117 million to build and includes 2,500 tonnes of steel.

About the Mascot

The Senators' mascot is a giant cat named Spartacat. He is 7 feet tall and weighs more than 300 pounds. He has long, bushy, red hair. Spartacat leads cheers and entertains fans. He draws Senators fans into the spirit of the game. As an added treat for fans, Spartacat uses a big air gun to shoot tin-foil–wrapped hot dogs into the crowd.

Hockey Positions

The positions in hockey are forward, defence, and goaltender. Each team is allowed six players on the ice. Teams usually play with three forwards, two defencemen, and one goaltender. The forwards include a right winger, left winger, and centre. The defensive pair is a right defender and a left defender.

The main job of all three forwards is to pass the puck up the ice and score goals. The centre generally takes the **face-off**. The right winger usually stays along the boards on the right side of the rink. The left winger does the same along the

left side. The centre generally plays between the two wingers and follows the puck. Daniel Alfredsson, Alexei Yashin, and Marion Hossa were all successful forwards with the Senators. Alfredsson is the Senators' all-time leader in games played, as well as in goals and assists. He was drafted by the Senators in the 1994 NHL **Entry Draft**. He has spent his entire NHL career with the team.

Defencemen try to prevent the **opposition** from scoring goals. They do this by staying between their goalie and the opposing players. They also force the opposition players out of good shooting positions whenever possible. Some defenders score goals and create scoring chances for their forwards. This type of defender is called an offensive defenceman. Wade Redden is a defenceman who has scored almost 400 points as a Senator.

SENATORS ALL-TIME LEADERS

Most Goals	**Most Games Played**
Daniel Alfredsson	Daniel Alfredsson
262 goals	706 games
Most Assists	**Most Penalty Minutes**
Daniel Alfredsson	Chris Neil
409 assists	776 **penalty** minutes
Most Points	**Most Goaltender Wins**
Daniel Alfredsson	Patrick Lalime
671 points	146 wins

The other type of defender is a stay-at-home defenceman, such as Chris Phillips. Stay-at-home defencemen rarely race up ice with the puck. Instead, they stay close to their goalie to prevent the other team from scoring.

The goalie's job is to stop the opposition from scoring. Goalies are the last line of defence. If they miss the puck, a goal is scored. Patrick Lalime played goal in Ottawa for many years. He played 283 games as a Senator and won 146 games of those games. Another former Senators goalie, Dominik Hasek, has won the Vezina Trophy as the NHL's best goalie six times throughout his career.

■■ **Following the 2005–2006 season, Dominik Hasek left the Senators to play for the Detroit Red Wings.**

The Goalie and his mask

Goalies express themselves through special designs on their masks. Ray Emery, one of the Senators' goalies, is a boxing fan. He has three masks painted with images of former boxing champions, including Marvin Hagler, Jack Johnson, and Mike Tyson.

There are two kinds of goalie masks currently used in the NHL. One is a helmet and cage combination, such as the mask worn by Dominik Hasek. However, most goalies wear a **fibreglass** mask that has a cage attached in the centre. They feel it provides more protection for the sides of the head. They also believe it will better absorb a slapshot.

As a child, Patrick Lalime liked to watch Looney Toons on television. He thought that Marvin the Martian looked like the Senators logo. An artist designed a Marvin the Martian image for Lalime's mask. Gold paint was then added to make the mask stand out.

Hockey Equipment

Hockey is a fast, rough sport. Players wear padded equipment to prevent injuries. Hockey equipment is like body armor. It includes helmets, padded gloves, knee-length padded pants, and loose, stretchy jerseys. Each jersey has the player's last name and number on the back. Players choose numbers that they like. They also select numbers that they think will bring them luck. Daniel Alfredsson wears number 11. He wore this number as a young soccer player in Sweden.

Players also wear shoulder pads, elbow pads, and thick socks with shin pads underneath. Some players wear a visor on their helmets to protect their eyes. Most Senators players wear visors. Chris Neil is a forward for the

Senators. He is one of the few players on the team that does not wear a visor.

Today's skates are made of leather and various plastic materials. Modern skates are more technologically advanced than older skates. They are also designed to be light. They allow players to turn more sharply and skate faster than they did before.

Goalies wear special equipment to protect them from hard shots. Some players fire the puck at more than 150 kilometres per hour.

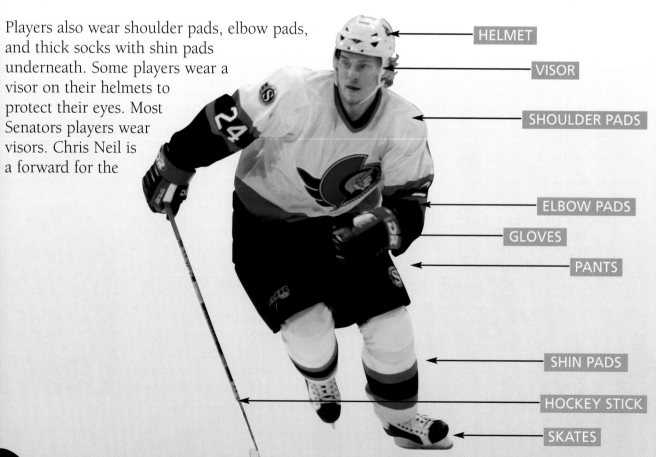

HELMET

VISOR

SHOULDER PADS

ELBOW PADS

GLOVES

PANTS

SHIN PADS

HOCKEY STICK

SKATES

Goaltenders wear thick pads that reach from their thighs to their skates. These pads are used to stop the puck from entering the net. Goaltenders use the pads to deflect the puck away from their net. They also wear a catcher or trapper on one hand and a blocker on the other. A goalie's catcher is similar to a baseball glove. Their blocker is a glove attached to a long, flat, padded surface. Goalies use the blocker to deflect the puck into the corner away from the net.

Team Jerseys

In the past, all hockey games were played on outdoor rinks. Players wore turtleneck sweaters and knitted wool caps to keep warm. Today, teams wear matching jerseys bearing their team logos.

The Ottawa Senators wear three different jerseys. Their home jersey is red with white and black trim. On the front of the jersey is a Roman **legionnaire**. The away jersey is very similar to the home jersey, except it is white with red and black trim.

From time to time at home games, the Senators wear their alternate, or third, jersey. This jersey is black with red, white, and gold strips. It also has black arrows around the gold trim.

GOALIE MASK

GOALIE STICK

GOALIE PADS

CATCHER

BLOCKER

Competing in the National Hockey League

There are currently 30 teams in the National Hockey League. Half of the teams play in the Eastern Conference. The other half play in the Western Conference. Each conference is made up of three divisions. In the Eastern Conference, the divisions include the Atlantic Division, the Northeast Division, and the Southeast Division, while in the Western Conference, the Central Division, the Northwest Division, and the Pacific Division are included.

Eight teams from each conference advance from the regular season to the playoffs. Playoff spots in the conference quarter finals are awarded on the basis of points earned during the regular season. Teams are **seeded** from #1 to #8 based on their regular-season points. Four series are then played with #1 playing #8, #2 playing #7, and so on. Each series is a best-of-seven format. The first team to win four games wins the series.

Winners of the conference quarter finals advance to the conference semifinals. The winning teams are then seeded in each series, based on the same criteria as the quarter finals. Winners of the semifinal series then advance to the conference finals. Conference winners play each other for the Stanley Cup.

■■ **The original Ottawa Senators won the Stanley Cup 10 times.**

WESTERN CONFERENCE

Central Division	**Northwest Division**	**Pacific Division**
CHICAGO BLACKHAWKS	🍁CALGARY FLAMES	ANAHEIM DUCKS
COLUMBUS BLUE JACKETS	COLORADO AVALANCHE	DALLAS STARS
DETROIT RED WINGS	🍁EDMONTON OILERS	LOS ANGELES KINGS
NASHVILLE PREDATORS	MINNESOTA WILD	PHOENIX COYOTES
ST. LOUIS BLUES	🍁VANCOUVER CANUCKS	SAN JOSE SHARKS

WESTERN CONFERENCE

| #1 versus #8 | #2 versus #7 |
| #3 versus #6 | #4 versus #5 |

QUARTER FINALS

EASTERN CONFERENCE

| #1 versus #8 | #2 versus #7 |
| #3 versus #6 | #4 versus #5 |

Top four teams move to next round

Top four teams move to next round

| #1 versus #4 |
| #2 versus #3 |

SEMIFINALS

| #1 versus #4 |
| #2 versus #3 |

Top two teams move to next round

Top two teams move to next round

| #1 versus #2 |

CONFERENCE FINALS

| #1 versus #2 |

Top team moves to last round

Top team moves to last round

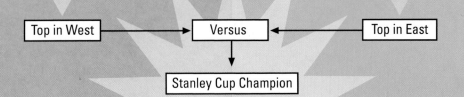

| Top in West | → | Versus | ← | Top in East |

Stanley Cup Champion

EASTERN CONFERENCE

Atlantic Division	**Northeast Division**	**Southeast Division**
NEW JERSEY DEVILS	BOSTON BRUINS	ATLANTA THRASHERS
NEW YORK ISLANDERS	BUFFALO SABRES	CAROLINA HURRICANES
NEW YORK RANGERS	🍁 MONTREAL CANADIENS	FLORIDA PANTHERS
PHILADELPHIA FLYERS	🍁 OTTAWA SENATORS	TAMPA BAY LIGHTNING
PITTSBURGH PENGUINS	🍁 TORONTO MAPLE LEAFS	WASHINGTON CAPITALS

The Battle of Ontario

The Ottawa Senators play in the Northeast Division of the Eastern Conference. They compete with the other teams in the conference for a playoff position. Their biggest **rival** in their division is the Toronto Maple Leafs. This is because more than just a playoff position is at stake when these two teams compete. Bragging rights for the province are also on the line.

This rivalry has become known as the Battle of Ontario. Players on both teams want to be known as the best in province. This makes players work extra hard to win when playing each other. Sometimes rivalries develop between individual players. Some individual battles can last for years.

Daniel Alfredsson from the Senators and Darcy Tucker from the Maple Leafs battled each other for years. This rivalry became intense during the 2002 Stanley Cup playoffs. During that series, Alfredsson checked Tucker into the boards, injuring Tucker's shoulder blade and dislocating his shoulder. The referee said it was a clean hit. Chris Neil from the Senators and Tie Domi from the Maple Leafs also battled each other for years. Both Neil and Domi are rugged players. They have fought each other many times

The Battle of Ontario is one of the best rivalries in hockey. So far, the Maple Leafs have won most of the battles. They have defeated the Senators in all three of the playoff series in which the two teams have played against each other.

The Battle of the Fans

The Senators rejoined the NHL in the 1992–93 season. Many people in Ottawa cheer for the Toronto Maple Leafs, even though they now have their own NHL team. One reason is because the Maple Leafs have been around for such a long time. Most Ottawa Senators fans live in or near Ottawa.

Making It to the NHL

Each year in June, the National Hockey League has a draft. It is called the NHL Entry Draft. During the Entry Draft, NHL teams select players from the Canadian Hockey League (CHL) and various **semi-professional** leagues around the world to play for them. Teams that finish low in the NHL regular season standings select first. Teams that finish high in the standings select last. This order helps balance the talent pool in the league.

Many players that are drafted have played in the CHL. This is a junior league made up of players between the ages of 16 to 20.

Sometimes drafted players are returned to the CHL to further develop their skills. Jason Spezza and Chris Phillips both returned to their CHL teams for one more year of development after being drafted by Ottawa. Daniel Alfredsson played in a professional league in Sweden for three years before joining the Senators.

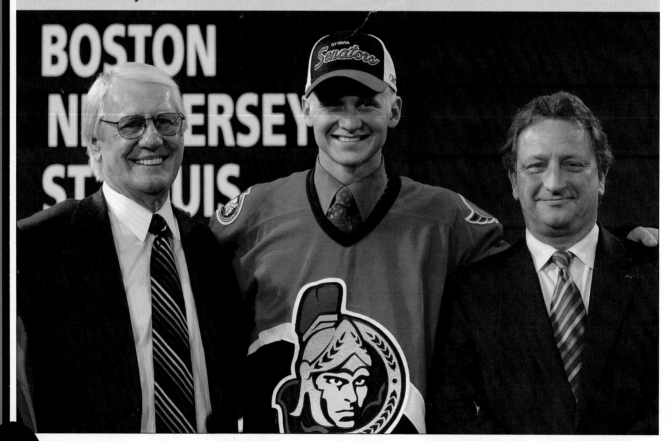

■ Defenceman Brian Lee is known for his excellent skating ability. Ottawa selected Lee ninth overall in the 2005 NHL Entry Draft.

By choosing early in the draft, teams often select talented young players that will help their teams in the future. The Senators have been able to select many first round draft picks for their team. This is because they finished near the bottom of the regular season standings for the first five years they were in the NHL.

Hockey players are sometimes traded to other teams for other players. They are also traded for draft choices. The Senators acquired defenceman Zdeno Chara in a trade with the New York Islanders.

NHL team **rosters** are made up of signed players. NHL teams sign the players that they think will give them the best chance of winning. In 2004, the Senators signed goalie Dominik Hasek. Signed players may be sent to the American Hockey League (AHL) for a while. The AHL is a semi-professional league. Most NHL franchises own an AHL team. The Birmingham Senators are Ottawa's AHL affiliate team. Players that are too old to play in the CHL are often sent to the AHL to develop their skills. Some players play for years in the AHL before getting an opportunity to play in the NHL. Jason Spezza played more than 120 games in the AHL. Today, he is one of the best forwards in the NHL.

Reporting on the Senators

**Reporting on the Senators
Gord Wilson and Dean Brown,
a Brilliant Broadcasting Team**

The experienced team of Dean Brown and Gord Wilson has been broadcasting the Senators' games since the team returned to the NHL in 1992. Brown provides play-by-play action. Wilson does the **colour commentary**. They announce the games each season on television and on the radio.

Gord Wilson

Dean Brown

19

The Olympics

Canadian Olympic Men's Hockey

The Canadian Olympic Men's hockey team is made up of the best hockey players of Canadian citizenship. NHL hockey fans from across the country cheer for them in the Olympics. The Canadian team's main rivals are Russia, the United States, the Czech Republic, Finland, and Sweden. Since 1920, Canada has won seven gold medals in Olympic hockey.

In the past, NHL players were not able to compete in the Winter Olympics. Canada would send amateur players to the games instead. In 1998, NHL players began to play on Canada's Olympic hockey team. Canada failed to capture a medal that year in Nagano, Japan. This was very disappointing for the team and for hockey fans across Canada. In 2002, Team Canada captured the gold medal in Salt Lake City, Utah. They defeated the United States in the gold medal game. Hockey fans from across Canada were delighted.

SENATORS PARTICIPATION ON TEAM CANADA
2006 Winter Olympics in Turin, Italy
Wade Redden, Dany Heatley
Jason Spezza (alternate)

Ottawa's head coach, Jacques Martin, was an assistant coach for the 2002 Team Canada Olympic squad that won a gold medal in Salt Lake City, Utah.

Canadian Olympic Women's Hockey

The Canadian Olympic Women's hockey team began competing in the Winter Olympics in 1998. Their team is made up of players from the National Women's Hockey League (NWHL). The Canadian women's team's biggest international rival is the United States. In 1998, Canada lost to the United States in the gold medal game. Hockey fans in Canada were devastated. However, Canada beat the U.S. team in the gold medal round in 2002 in Salt Lake City, Utah. Then, in 2006, they beat Sweden in Turin, Italy, to again capture the gold medal. The team has been led by star forwards Cassie Campbell and Hayley Wickenheiser. Wickenheiser is the only woman to ever score a goal in a professional men's hockey league game.

■ The Canadian Olympic Women's hockey team outscored their opponents 28–0 in their first two round-robin games of the 2006 Olympics in Turin, Italy.

Popular Senators Coaches

Rick Bowness

In the fall of 1992, Rick Bowness was the head coach of the Ottawa Senators. The team had just rejoined the NHL after an absence of more than 55 years. Although Ottawa did not make the playoffs under his leadership, he is the only NHL head coach to spend the first three seasons behind the bench of an expansion team. Prior to joining the Senators, Bowness coached the Boston Bruins to the Wales, or Eastern, Conference Finals in the 1991–1992 season. After leaving the Ottawa Senators in 1995, he went on to coach the New York Islanders and the Phoenix Coyotes.

Jacques Martin

Jacques Martin was born in 1952 in St. Pascal, Ontario. Jacques Martin never played for the NHL during his hockey career. His coaching career began in the Ontario Hockey League. He coached the Peterborough Petes and then the Guelph Platers. His NHL coaching career began with the St. Louis Blues. He won a Stanley Cup in 1996 when he was the assistant coach of the Colorado Avalanche. That same year, Martin became head coach for the Senators. He was known for his laid-back, soft-spoken style. Most NHL coaches are loud and enthusiastic. Martin believes that the best teams are good defenders. His teams are known for their tight-checking defensive style of play. Martin is well-respected in the NHL for his knowledge of the game. He won the Jack Adams Award for top NHL coach in 1999. In 2004, Martin became head coach of the Florida Panthers.

Bryan Murray

In 2004, Bryan Murray took over the head coaching duties of the Ottawa Senators from Jacques Martin. Murray's coaching career began with Pembroke of the Canadian Junior Hockey League. Next, he coached the Regina Pats of the Canadian Hockey League. The Pats made it to the Memorial Cup. Murray then moved to the American Hockey League, where he coached the Hershey Bears. He won coach of the year in the AHL. Murray's first coaching job in the

NHL was for the Washington Capitals. While coaching this team, he won the Jack Adams Award in 1984. Murray coached the Capitals from 1982 to 1990. He went on to coach the Anaheim Mighty Ducks, the Florida Panthers, and the Detroit Red Wings. Since Murray became the head coach of the Ottawa Senators, they have become a successful team in the league.

Making the Call

As well as coaches and players, the NHL needs game officials. Game officials are linesmen and referees. Linesmen call **offsides** and **icing**, while referees call most of the penalties. Referees need to be good skaters because they have to keep up with the play for an entire game. Unlike hockey players, referees are not able to rest between **shifts**.

Referees are so important to hockey that several have been inducted into the Hockey Hall of Fame. You can read about them on the Hockey Hall of Fame website at *www.legendsofhockey.net*.

The first step to becoming a referee is to contact a local league office. Training is available at officiating schools, such as the North American School of Officiating in Guelph, Ontario. These schools teach ice positioning, signals, penalty calling, skating skills, and off-ice theory.

A referee needs all of these skills so that he or she can make the right calls during a game. Every year, referees attend a week-long training camp. During the camp, fitness level and skating ability are tested. At the end of the week, referees leave camp and head to their first game of the season.

Unforgettable Moments

During the 2002–03 season, the Ottawa Senators finished the regular season with 113 points. They were awarded the President's Trophy as the NHL's best team. This was the first time they had achieved this much success since rejoining the league. During the playoffs, the Senators advanced to the Eastern Conference finals. It was the first time they had made it that far in the playoffs. This was also the first time they had performed better than the Toronto Maple Leafs in the playoffs. However, the Senators lost in the seventh game of the conference finals to the New Jersey Devils. The Devils went on to capture the Stanley Cup.

The NHL rules were changed in the 2005–06 season. Hockey games could no longer end in a tie. If a game is tied at the end of regulation time, a five-minute overtime period is played. Each team is allowed only four players plus a goalie on the ice during overtime. If overtime does not produce a winner, the game is decided by a shootout.

In their season-opening game on October 5, 2005, the Ottawa Senators and Toronto Maple Leafs were tied 2–2 after 65 minutes of play.

Goaltenders Patrick Lalime of the Senators and Martin Brodeur of the New Jersey Devils battled a seven game series in the 2003 Eastern Conference finals.

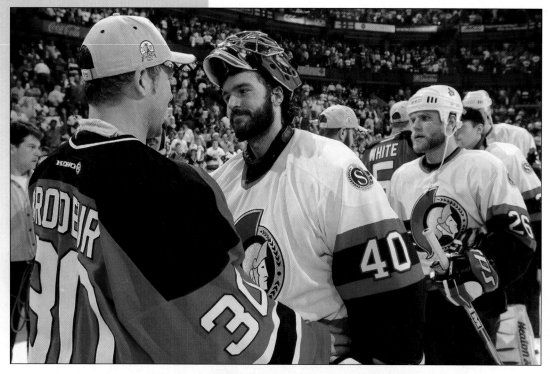

They became the first teams in NHL history to decide the outcome of a game in a shootout.

In the shootout, Daniel Alfredsson recorded the game-deciding goal, while Dany Heatley also slid the puck past Toronto's Ed Belfour. Alfredsson and Heatley made NHL history.

They became the first players in the history of the league to win a hockey game with a shootout goal. To record this historic event, their sticks were sent to the Hockey Hall of Fame.

NHL INDIVIDUAL AND TEAM AWARDS WON BY THE SENATORS		
Name of Award	**Awarded to**	**Senators Winners**
Art Ross Trophy	the player with the most points during the regular season	Punch Broadbent, 1922 Cy Denneny, 1924
Hart Memorial Trophy	the most valuable player	Frank Nighbor, 1924
Lady Byng Trophy	the player who best combines hockey skill, sportsmanship, and gentlemanly conduct	Frank Nighbor, 1925, 1926
Calder Trophy	the best rookie, or first-year player	Daniel Alfredsson, 1996
Jack Adams Award	the coach deemed most influential to the team's success	Jacques Martin, 1999
President's Trophy	the best team during the regular season	Ottawa Senators, 2002–03
Prince of Wales Trophy	the regular season champions of the American Division of the NHL between 1924 and 1938	Ottawa Senators, 1927

Senators Legends and Current Stars

#11 Daniel Alfredsson

CAREER FACTS

Daniel Alfredsson was selected in the fifth round of the 1994 NHL Entry Draft by the Ottawa Senators. He won the Calder Trophy in 1995 as the league's best first-year player. He is the current leader of the team in games played, and in goals, assists, and total points. Many consider Alfredsson to be one of Ottawa's best forwards. He plays on a line with Dany Heatley and Jason Spezza. This line contributed a total of 112 goals and 184 assists to the team during the 2005–06 regular season. As well, Alfredsson won a gold medal with Sweden at the Winter Olympics in Turin, Italy, in 2006.

Position Right Wing
Born December 11, 1972

Hometown
Bergsjon Goteborg,
Sweden

#4 Chris Phillips

CAREER FACTS

Chris Phillips was drafted first overall in the 1996 NHL Entry Draft by the Ottawa Senators. The club drafted him first because they felt he was the best 18-year old player available to help their team. He is a tough defender. He is also very steady and dependable at protecting his goalie.

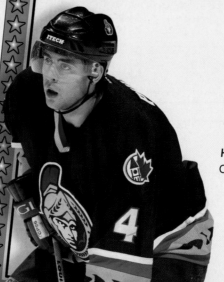

Position Defence
Born March 9, 1978

Hometown
Calgary, Alberta

26

#6 Wade Redden

CAREER FACTS

Wade Redden was chosen second overall in the 1995 NHL Entry Draft by the New York Islanders. He was then traded to the Ottawa Senators for Bryan Berard. The Senators had chosen Berard first overall in the same Entry Draft. Since then, Redden has been an effective defenceman for the Senators. His team relies on him in key situations to prevent the opposing team from scoring. In 2006, he was chosen to play for the Canadian Olympic Team.

Position Defence
Born June 12, 1977

Hometown
Lloydminster,
Saskatchewan

Daniel Alfredsson said this about selecting his jersey number: "I had two choices when I picked my number—22 and 11. Eleven was the number I had when I played soccer, so it was an easy choice."

Wade Redden said this about scoring a big NHL goal: "I scored a number of big goals in junior to tie some playoff games. I also scored a big goal in the World Junior Championships. But those goals were in junior. This one is a lot different. It's the NHL."

#19 Jason Spezza

CAREER FACTS

At the age of 15, Jason Spezza became the youngest player ever to play in the Ontario Hockey League all-star game. In the 2001 NHL Entry Draft, Ottawa selected Jason as the second overall pick in the draft. In the 2005-2006 season, Spezza started off with a bang, scoring 22 points in his first 11 games. He ended the season strong, finishing with 90 points.

Position Centre
Born June 13, 1983

Hometown
Toronto, Ontario

The Best Years

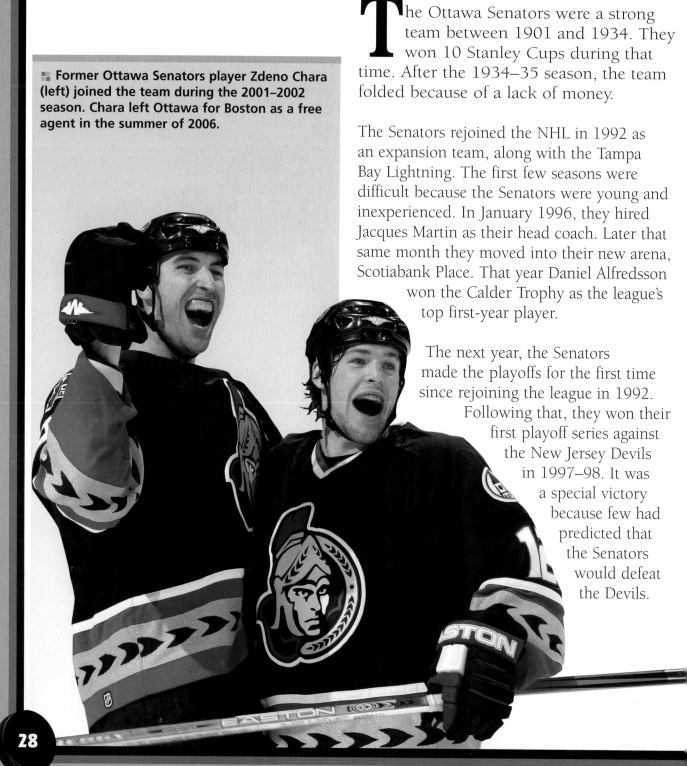

■■ Former Ottawa Senators player Zdeno Chara (left) joined the team during the 2001–2002 season. Chara left Ottawa for Boston as a free agent in the summer of 2006.

The Ottawa Senators were a strong team between 1901 and 1934. They won 10 Stanley Cups during that time. After the 1934–35 season, the team folded because of a lack of money.

The Senators rejoined the NHL in 1992 as an expansion team, along with the Tampa Bay Lightning. The first few seasons were difficult because the Senators were young and inexperienced. In January 1996, they hired Jacques Martin as their head coach. Later that same month they moved into their new arena, Scotiabank Place. That year Daniel Alfredsson won the Calder Trophy as the league's top first-year player.

The next year, the Senators made the playoffs for the first time since rejoining the league in 1992. Following that, they won their first playoff series against the New Jersey Devils in 1997–98. It was a special victory because few had predicted that the Senators would defeat the Devils.

In the 1999–2000 season, the Senators were involved in a contract dispute with their star forward, Alexei Yashin. Yashin wanted more money than the Senators were willing to pay. He did not play for the entire season. However, the Senators finished the regular season in second place with 93 points. In 2001, the Senators traded Yashin to the New York Islanders for Zdeno Chara, Bill Muckalt, and the Islanders first-round pick in the NHL Entry Draft. The Senators used the draft pick to acquire Jason Spezza. Chara and Spezza were key players that helped the Senators win the President's Trophy in 2003.

In the 2005–06 season, the Senators had one of the more talented teams in the NHL. Dominik Hasek was in goal. He is one of the best goalies to ever play the game. On defence they had Chara and Wade Redden. Chara is the biggest player in the NHL. He stands 6-foot-9 inches tall and weights 260 pounds. He delivers hard body checks. Wade Redden is very skilled on defence. He seldom makes errors and delivers skillful passes to move the puck out of the defensive zone. He also possesses excellent play-making ability on the **power play**. The Senators had one of the best forward lines in hockey. It featured Alfredsson, Heatley, and Spezza. In 2005–06, Alfredsson and Heatley tied for fourth in league scoring with 103 points each. Heatley became the first Senators player to score 50 goals in a single season. Jason Spezza finished second overall in the league with 71 assists. Most of those assists were the result of goals scored by Alfredsson and Heatley.

■ **Dany Heatley joined the Senators during the 2005–2006 season.**

SENATORS IN THE COMMUNITY

The Ottawa Senators contribute to their community in many positive ways. The Senators have created an organization called the Ottawa Senators Foundation. This foundation raises money for various organizations and charities. Some of these include the Boys and Girls Club, the Children's Hospital of Eastern Ontario, and the Juvenile Diabetes Foundation. The foundation also provides money for students who cannot afford to pay for their college or university classes in eastern Ontario and western Quebec.

Quiz

1 Where and when was the first hockey game played?

2 How many teams play in the NHL?

3 When did the NHL begin?

4 What is the name of the Ottawa Senators' home arena?

5 Which Ottawa Senators coach never played for the NHL?

6 What is the name of the Ottawa Senators' mascot?

7 How many teams were in the NHL when it first formed in 1917?

8 Who are the Ottawa Senators' biggest rivals?

9 Which player with the Ottawa Senators won a gold medal with Sweden at the 2006 Winter Olympics in Turin, Italy?

10 Which players with the Ottawa Senators were members of Team Canada at the 2006 Winter Olympics?

Answers

1. The first hockey game was played at the Victoria Skating rink in Montreal in 1875.
2. Thirty teams play in the NHL today.
3. The NHL began in 1917.
4. The Senators' home arena is Scotiabank Place.
5. Jacques Martin never played in the NHL.
6. Spartacat is the Senators' mascot.
7. There were four teams in the NHL.
8. The Toronto Maple Leafs are the Senators' biggest rivals.
9. Daniel Alfredsson won a gold medal.
10. Dany Heatley, Wade Redden, and Jason Spezza were members of Team Canada.

Further Research

Many books and websites have been established to provide information on the Ottawa Senators. To learn more about the Senators, borrow books from the library, or surf the Internet.

— BOOKS TO READ —

ost libraries have computers that connect to a database for researching information.
you input a key word, you will be provided with a list of books in the library that contain
ormation on that topic. Non-fiction books are arranged numerically, using their call number.
tion books are organized alphabetically by the author's last name.

— ONLINE SITES —

search for books about the Ottawa Senators, type key words, such as "Ottawa Senators"
"NHL teams," in the search field.

www.ottawasenatorsfoundation.com

www.ottawasenators.com

www.legendsofhockey.net

Glossary

amateur: a player who is not a professional and plays a sport for the pleasure of it without being paid money to play

colour commentary: the analysis, strategy, and statistics of a game provided by a broadcaster when there is a stoppage in play

entry draft: a process used by NHL teams to select new players

face-off: when the referee drops the puck between two players to start the play

fibreglass: glass drawn and spun into fine threads

franchises: teams or organizations that become members of a league

Great Depression: the time between 1929 and 1934 when business was bad and many people lost their jobs

Hockey Hall of Fame: a place where former players and people involved in hockey are honored for their contributions to the game

icing: a stoppage in play caused by a player shooting the puck from his or her side of the centre line to the opposition's goal line without it being touched

legionnaire: a Roman soldier

offsides: stoppages in play caused by a player crossing the offensive blue line before the puck

opposition: a team that opposes another team

penalty: a punishment for breaking a rule of the game

playoffs: a final game or series of games played to decide who will be champion

power play: a situation where one team has more players on the ice than the other team due to penalties

professional: earning a living from a sport

rival: a competitor

rosters: lists of players playing on a team

seeded: being placed in a specific rank or position

semi-professional: a player who plays for money, but is paid less than what professionals are paid

shifts: groups of players taking turns with other groups of players while playing a game

Stanley Cup: the National Hockey League's prize for the best team in the playoffs

Index